COURAGE

by Jane Belk Moncure
illustrated by Helen Endres

THE
CHILD'S
WORLD

ELGIN, ILLINOIS 60120

Distributed by Childrens Press, 1224 West Van Buren Street, Chicago, Illinois 60607.

Library of Congress Cataloging in Publication Data

Moncure, Jane Belk.
    Courage.

    (What is it?)
    SUMMARY: Presents various situations that exemplify the nature of courage.
    1. Courage—Juvenile literature. (1. Courage)
I. Endres, Helen. II. Title
BJ1533.C8M66 1981   179'.6   80-39515
ISBN 0-89565-202-1

COURAGE

What is courage?

Getting back on a bicycle after you
have fallen off, that's courage!

Letting a doctor give you a shot, even
though it stings, that's courage.

Courage is telling a big boy not to
tease your little brother.

Practicing a dive off the diving board, even though you didn't do it very well the first time, that's courage. Courage is doing something till you get it right!

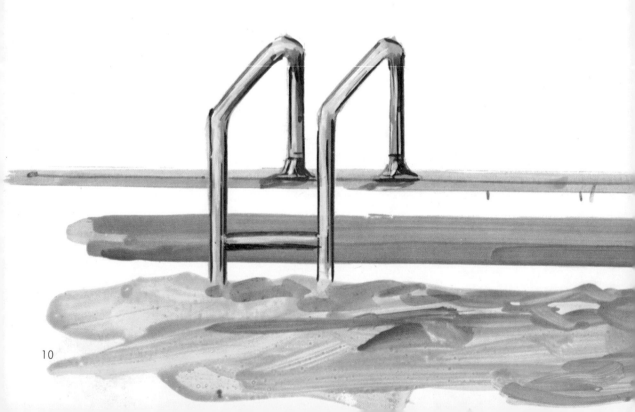

Courage is talking things over with Dad when you've done something wrong.

Courage is saying, "I'm sorry," when you fight with your best friend. Courage is making things right again.

Telling mother you dried your dirty
hands on the clean towel, that's courage.

When you make the last out in a baseball game, courage is not blaming the umpire!

When a friend wants to copy your
paper, courage is saying, "No."

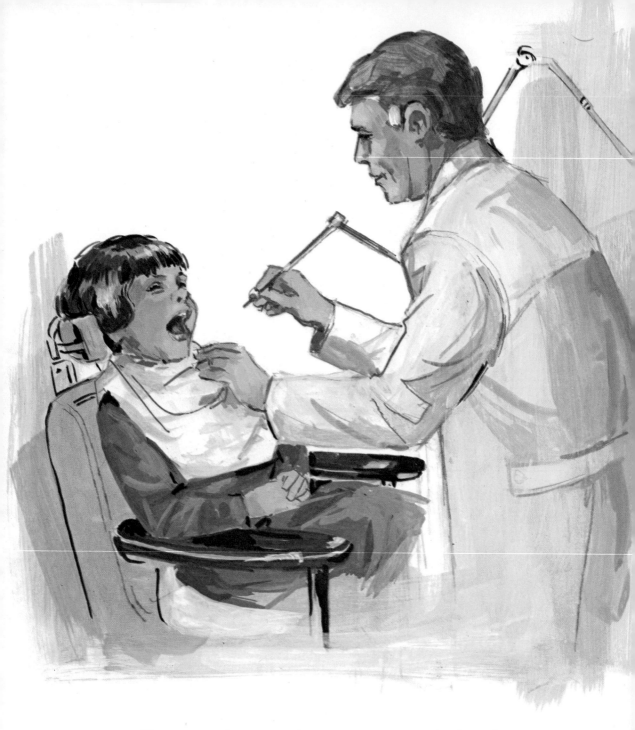

Courage is opening your mouth for the dentist.

Courage is learning to pat the
neighbor's big dog—after Mother has
said he's friendly.

Courage is going off cheerfully for your first day at a new school.

Letting your parents go for a week-end
holiday while you stay with friends,
that's courage.

Courage is climbing the ladder to slide down the slide.

When you meet new people, courage is
being the first to say, ''Hi.''

Courage is trying to be the best kind
of person you can be, every day.

Can you think of other ways to show courage?

About the Author:

Jane Belk Moncure, author of many books and stories for young children, is a graduate of Virginia Commonwealth University and Columbia University. She has taught nursery, kindergarten and primary children in Europe and America. Mrs. Moncure has taught early childhood education while serving on the faculties of Virginia Commonwealth University and the University of Richmond. She was the first president of the Virginia Association for Early Childhood Education and has been recognized widely for her services to young children. She is married to Dr. James A. Moncure, Vice President of Elon College, and currently lives in Burlington, North Carolina.

About the Artist:

Helen Endres is a commercial artist, designer and illustrator of children's books. She has lived and worked in the Chicago area since coming from her native Oklahoma in 1952. Graduated from Tulsa University with a BA, she received further training at Hallmark in Kansas City and from the Chicago Art Institute. Ms. Endres attributes much of her creative achievement to the advice and encouragement of her Chicago contemporaries and to the good humor and patience of the hundreds of young models who have posed for her.